THE NEW
My Writing Book

By _____
Write your name here.

By Joyce C. Bumgardner
Illustrated by David LaRochelle

FROGGIE PRESS
Plymouth, Minnesota

This book is dedicated to young writers everywhere who have important things to say, who are filled with wonderful ideas, thoughts and dreams. Thanks to all my cheerleaders who kept saying, "You can do it!" and to teachers everywhere who help students discover and develop their competency in writing.

Thanks to students who tested and approved writing projects in *The New My Writing Book*.

Special thanks to Karin B. Miller, chief advisor and book designer.

No part of this publication may be reproduced in whole or in part, or stored in a retrieval system, or transmitted in any form or by any means, electronic, mechanical, photocopying, recording, or otherwise, without written permission of the author and publisher.

ISBN 0-9624260-1-6

Copyright 1998 Joyce C. Bumgardner
All rights reserved.
Published by Froggie Press

Printed in the U.S.A.

You can write in this book!

Write stories...funny letters...important notices...secret thoughts...great new ideas...

Each page gives you an idea to write about. Choose any page you like—you don't have to start at the beginning. Write a little or a lot.

Exercise your imagination! You may find yourself writing things you never thought you could write.

When you're finished, you will have your own book to read over and over again. You may want to share some of it with your family and friends.

* Throughout the book, you will find advice to writers, marked with *. Read and think about these ideas. They will help you become a stronger writer.

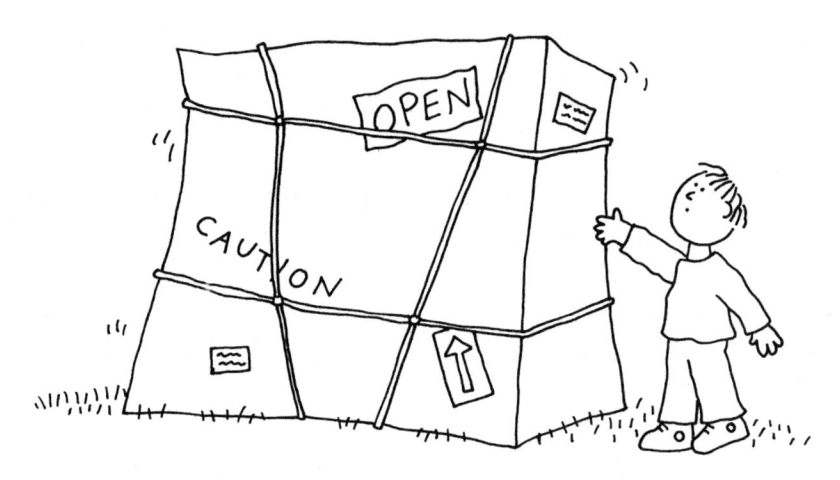

Imagine this! You have just come home from school. Sitting in your front yard is a huge, mysterious box. It's bigger than a refrigerator, bigger than the front door of your school. A note on the box says, *Open slowly and carefully.* No one else is at home. It is up to you to open the box. What do you think is inside? How will you open it? Then what happens? Strange noises are coming from inside the box.

I got up, ate breakfast and went to school. I went home and played, had dinner, watched TV and went to bed.

This is not a story. A story needs a *bump* in it! A *bump* is when something *happens*. In the story of *Goldilocks and the Three Bears,* there is a *bump* when snoopy Goldilocks enters the bears' house. There are *bumps* when she eats the porridge and breaks Little Bear's chair. The biggest *bump* is when the bears come home and wake Goldilocks. She jumps out of bed, runs through the doorway and never comes back.

Bumps are funny, scary, exciting or even sad happenings in your story. They're often what we describe as the best parts of a story.

One night I went for a walk. I saw birds in the trees and cars going up and down the street. My neighbor's dog watched me from their front porch. I saw dirt on the streets from melting snow. The trees were covered with leaves. Then I got tired, so I went home. The end.

This is boring! It has no *bumps* in it. Turn it into a lively story by adding someone doing stunts on a skateboard, or an elephant galloping down the street, or someone dropping candy from a hot air balloon flying overhead. Put in some excitement, something funny or scary or adventuresome. Add some *bumps*!

_____

_____

_____

_____

_____

_____

_____

_____

_____

_____

_____

* When you have finished your story, cover your ears firmly with your hands flat against your head and read it aloud, softly, to yourself. Listen to it. Where do you hear bumps? Writers must listen to what they write to know how their stories sound. Sometimes they change their stories to make them stronger.

***O**ne day I went fishing. I caught some fish. Then I went home and had dinner. It was good.*

This story has no *bumps*. Make it your own by adding some excitement, some action. What was the biggest fish you caught? Did it fight to get away? What did you do?

_____

_____

_____

_____

_____

_____

_____

_____

_____

_____

_____

_____

* Cover your ears and read your story aloud; listen to it—be your own audience. How does it sound? Did you make any changes? Hearing our writing out loud often shows us where we can add or delete words to make it better. Sometimes you will cross out or change whole sentences.

Imagine this: Walking to school one morning, you find a $10 bill on the sidewalk. How do you feel? What are you thinking? What will you do with the money?

* *Writers need minds that are open to new ways of thinking, to new ways of seeing. They must be able to look at things from more than one point of view.*

Now imagine this: When you arrive at school one morning, you discover that you have lost a $10 bill. How do you feel? What are you thinking? What will you do?

_____

_____

_____

_____

_____

_____

_____

_____

_____

_____

_____

Writing about things from different points of view makes us think more clearly about how thoughts and feelings change, depending on one's situation.

Think of another happening that could be seen in more than one way. Write about it from two points of view. For example, be a teacher giving a test, then a student taking the test. Write from the point of view of a kid with a messy room, then from the point of view of a mom or dad who would like it to be neat. Or—you decide on two different points of view. Then write them.

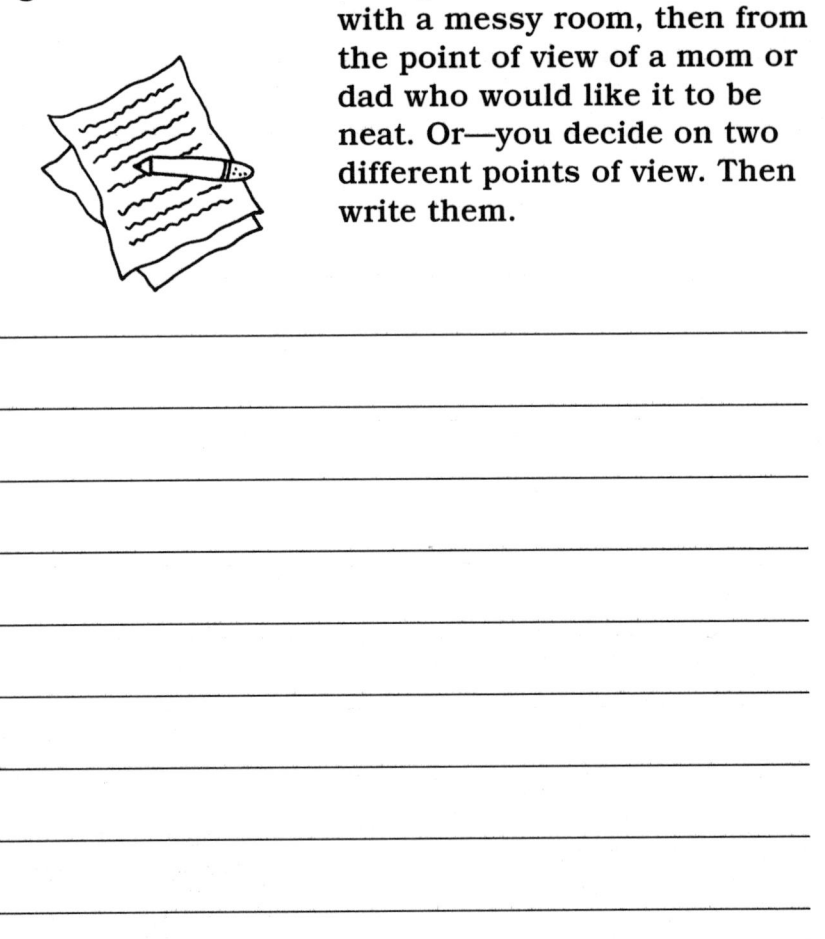

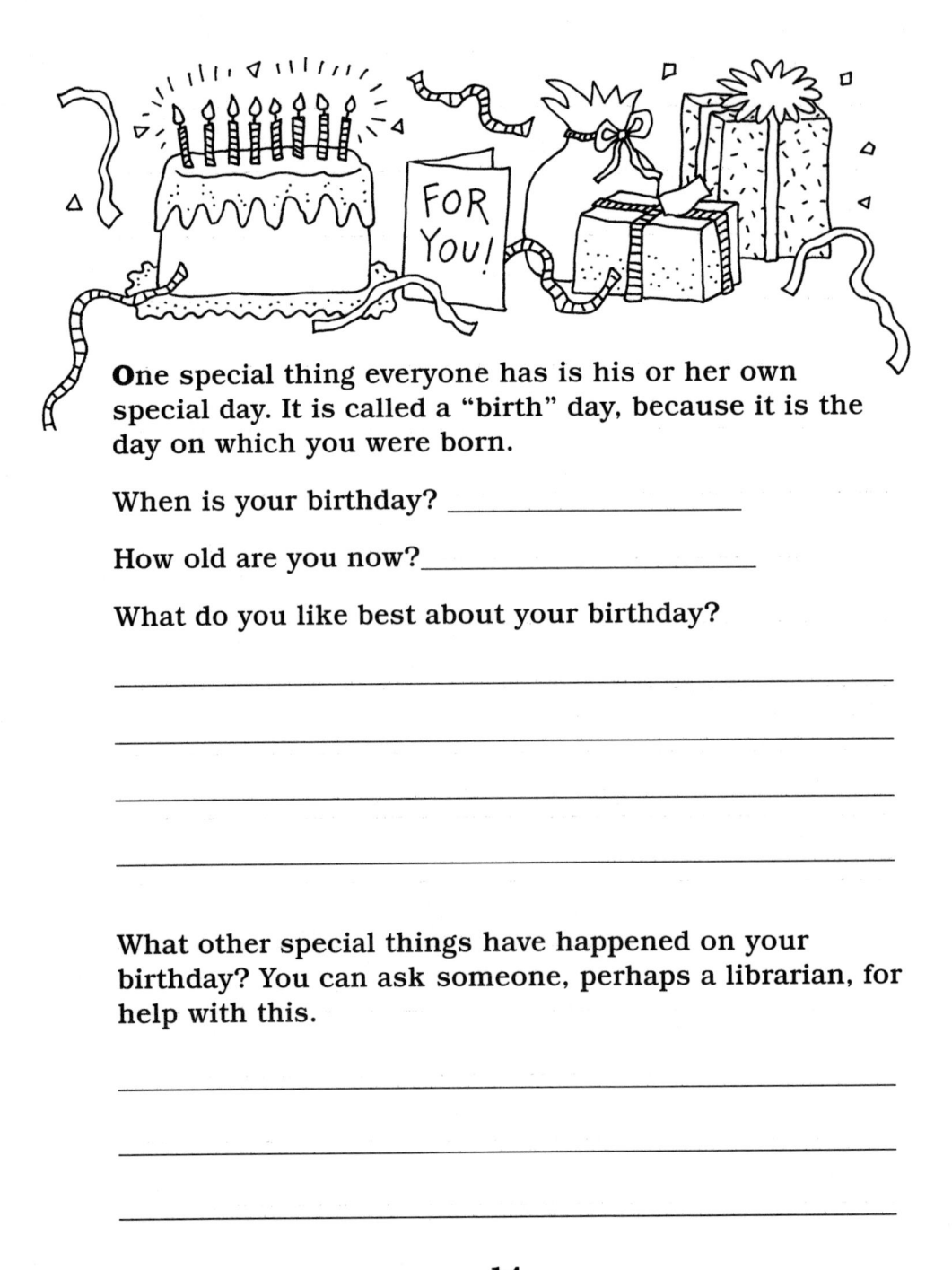

One special thing everyone has is his or her own special day. It is called a "birth" day, because it is the day on which you were born.

When is your birthday? _____

How old are you now? _____

What do you like best about your birthday?

_____
_____
_____
_____

What other special things have happened on your birthday? You can ask someone, perhaps a librarian, for help with this.

_____
_____
_____

Each birthday you celebrate means you are growing older. What are some of your favorite things to do now?

_____

_____

_____

_____

When you celebrate your next birthday, will you be able to do something that you couldn't do before? What is it? Write about it.

_____

_____

_____

_____

What do you dream of doing some day?

_____

_____

_____

_____

Sometimes, when rain is falling hard and fast, people say it is *raining cats and dogs*. Wouldn't that be funny! On a day when you don't like the weather, write your own forecast. Maybe it will be snowing white goose feathers or raining chocolate syrup. You decide. For once you can order just the kind of weather you like.

_____

_____

_____

_____

_____

_____

_____

_____

_____

_____

Stories sometimes tell about magic lamps and genies who grant wishes. If you could wish for three things, what would they be? You cannot wish for extra wishes! Think before you begin to write.

When you open the door and step outside your house, you see and hear many things. Do it: open your door and go outside. Find just one special thing and look at it carefully. What is it? How big is it? Does it make sounds? What color is it? What shape is it? Does it have a smell? Examine it carefully.

Now go back inside. Write about the thing you chose. Tell everything you know about it. When you are finished, ask someone to read what you wrote. Can your reader "see" what you described after reading your description?

_____

_____

_____

_____

_____

_____

_____

_____

* *Writers paint pictures by using words that tell what we see, hear, feel, smell and taste. This is called description. Tell about colors, sizes and shapes.*

Some trees are short and some are tall. Pretend that you are sitting in the top of a tall tree, looking down at what is around and below you. What do you see? How do you feel?

_____

_____

_____

_____

_____

_____

_____

_____

All hands are different. There are old hands and young hands, small and large hands, and hands of many colors. There are hands wearing jewelry and hands worn from hard work.

Close your eyes. Picture a pair of hands: see them in your mind's eye (your imagination). Examine the fingers, the nails. Whose hands are they?

Write about the hands. You might begin by saying, *These are my grandmother's hands* or *These are my sister's hands.* Tell everything you can about these hands—paint a picture with words. What can they do? How do they look?

_____

_____

_____

_____

_____

_____

_____

Sometimes it is nice to be home alone. You can run up and down the stairs and all through the house, sing as loudly as you want, and eat all the cookies in the cookie jar!

What do you like to do when you are all alone?

_____

_____

_____

_____

_____

_____

_____

_____

_____

_____

Books are full of wonderful things. Sometimes you learn about new places. Sometimes you meet new friends. Sometimes you read about things that really happen; other times, you read about things that only happen in make-believe.

Think about a favorite book. Who is the author? What happened in the story? Why is it a favorite? Why do you think the author wrote the book as he or she did?

Write about the book. Maybe writing about it will make you want to read it again.

_____

_____

_____

_____

Whatever your age, you know many things. Think about some of the things you know and write about them.

Examples:
I know that frogs eat bugs and help our environment.
I know that kernels explode into popcorn.
I know that houses are built from the foundation up.

_____

_____

_____

_____

_____

_____

_____

_____

_____

_____

Fresh bread baking; newly-washed earth after a rain; a favorite perfume or cologne; all of these are special smells.

What are some of your favorite smells? Write about them here.

_____

_____

_____

_____

_____

_____

_____

_____

_____

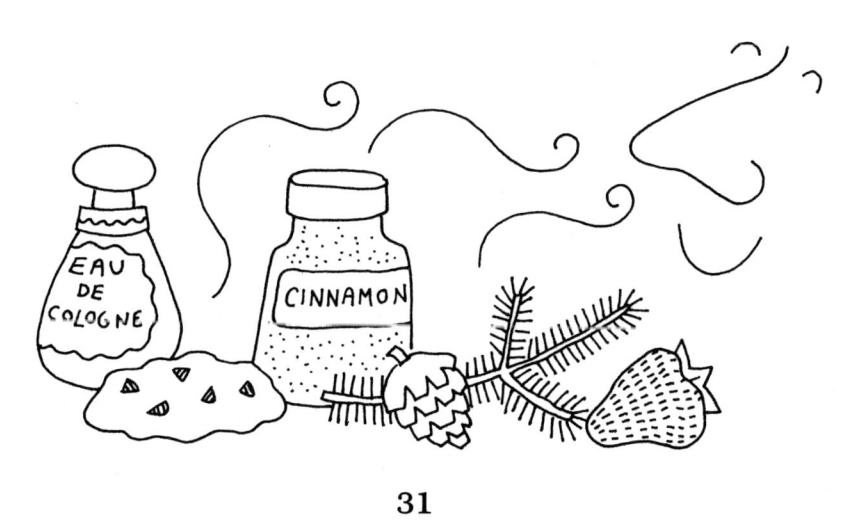

_____
_____
_____
_____
_____
_____
_____
_____
_____

There are many things you might want to be when you grow up. Maybe you want to start thinking about it now. You might want to be a teacher, a radio announcer, a fishing guide, an engineer or a pilot. You might be a forest ranger, a farmer, a doctor, or a computer programmer. Or how about a high-wire trapeze artist, a cartoonist, a musician, or the president of the United States? Think about it. Now write about it.

_____

_____

_____

_____

_____

_____

If you enjoy writing about things like this, you might want to be a writer when you grow up!

Inventors create new things that people need and want. Thomas Edison invented over 1,000 items, including the phonograph and the light bulb. Research by Gertrude Elion led to the invention of many important medicines. And Lonnie Johnson invented the Super Soaker squirt gun, one of the world's most popular toys. You can be an inventor, too. Write about something you think people need. What is it? How will it work? Why would people like to use it?

Draw a picture of your invention here.

What is your favorite food? Is it a huge piece of cheesy pizza? Fluffy popcorn with lots of butter? Is it chocolate cake with lots of chocolate frosting? A big, crisp, red apple? Think about it.

Now write a letter to your favorite kind of food. Tell it how much you like it, why it is your favorite food, and anything else you might want to say.

Dear Yummy_____,

_____

_____

_____

_____

_____

_____

_____

_____

Write about some of your other favorite foods. What are they? Who prepares them? What do you like best about them? Why do you like them? If they're part of a family tradition, write about that too.

Reporters interview people to learn new information. They ask questions, then write about what they learn. You can be a reporter, too. Ask your mother or dad, your grandmother or grandfather, to tell you about things they liked to do when they were your age. Ask about best friends, the houses where they lived, their pets and favorite games. Jot down some notes while you do your interview.

Write here about what you have learned.

_____

_____

_____

_____

_____

_____

_____

Imagine this! Your name is drawn in a store's contest and you've just come home with all kinds of great prizes: a tent, a new red dirt bike, a canoe, a year's supply of free movie tickets, a lifetime supply of popcorn and more.

Write a letter to the store. Tell how much you like your prizes, which is your favorite, and how you felt when your learned you had won.
Be sure to say thank you.

Dear _____,

_____

_____

_____

_____

_____

_____

Sometimes, if you write to tell a company that you really liked what they made, they will answer your letter and maybe even send you a free sample. Choose one of your favorite products. Find the company's address on the package. Then write a letter to tell them how much you like the product. Check for correct spelling, punctuation and neatness. Read it aloud to yourself before sending it.

Sometimes it's necessary to apologize. Imagine this: You have just returned from having lunch with the Queen of Kookamunga. Unfortunately, you knocked a big pot of cherry jam into her lap and it got all over her royal robes. When she tried to clean it off, she got it on her face and in her hair.

You got the giggles. You told her, "Thank you for the lunch," and left in a terrible hurry. Now you want to write her a letter of apology.

Dear Queen,

_____

_____

_____

_____

_____

_____

_____

_____

_____

_____

_____

_____

Changing things can make you feel you've accomplished something. For example, you know that throwing bottles, cans and Styrofoam cups along roads or in lakes causes pollution. (When people do this, we call them *litterbugs*. It is not good to be one of these!)

A good way to remind people to stop doing this and to help keep our earth clean is to write a notice about it and put it where others can see it.

Write a notice about something you would like to change. Tell what you want to change, why you want the change, and how you think it should be done.

NOTICE! NOTICE! NOTICE! NOTICE!

If you could be an animal, which one would you choose? An elephant? A red cardinal? A cocker spaniel? What would you eat? How would you move around? Where would you live? Who would be your friends? Where would you go in winter? What would you do to stay cool during hot summers? What color would you be? Would you have fur? Feathers? Scales? Wings? Would you be big or small?

Write about it here.

_____

_____

_____

_____

_____

_____

_____

_____

Each of us has a "secret me" inside. There are things you wish you could do, places you would like to go, ideas that no one else knows. Write about the secret *you*. When you finish, you might want to paste a piece of paper over what you wrote so it still will be a secret.

_____

_____

_____

_____

_____

_____

_____

_____

_____

_____

_____
_____
_____
_____
_____
_____
_____
_____
_____
_____
_____
_____
_____

Sometimes friends move away. Maybe you have had to move. If this has happened to you, write about it. If you moved, where did you move? How did you feel about moving? Did you help pack your family's things? How did you make friends in your new neighborhood? Did anyone come to welcome you? How did it feel to attend a new school?

If a friend moved away, how did you and your friend feel about the move? Did you do something special with your friend before he or she left? What did you do to remain friends after the move?

_____

_____

_____

_____

_____

_____

_____

_____

Money can be used for many things. It can buy things you need and things you want. It can pay for you to travel. It can be used to help other people.

Imagine that you have just earned a lot of money. Think about what you might do with it. Write about it.

_____

_____

_____

_____

_____

_____

_____

_____

_____

Imagine this! One day while you are walking along the beach, a friendly gray whale swims up and invites you to climb on its back for a ride. You slip and slide as you climb onto your new friend. Then...

Write about it. Where do you go? What do you see? How does it feel? What do you hear?

_____

_____

_____

_____

_____

_____

_____

_____

_____

_____

_____

How do you feel when you are back on dry land?

_____

_____

_____

_____

_____

When we give directions to someone, we must give the directions in the correct order. Otherwise, the cookies might not taste good, or our friend might never get to where he's going, or the model she wants to build might look strange when it's finished!

Write out the directions for making a sandwich—your favorite kind. Use these words: *first, next* and *then.*

Directions for _____

_____

First_____

_____

_____

Next_____

_____

_____

Then_____

_____

_____

_____

Now give directions for doing something else. When you finish writing, read the directions aloud to yourself. Have you told everything that someone else will need to know?

_____

_____

_____

_____

_____

_____

_____

Many people like to travel. Often so much happens on a trip that we can't remember it all.

A good way to remember is to keep a travel journal. In it, you can write important and special things that happen. If you write a little bit each day, it will help you remember much of your trip when you are back home.

Write about a real or pretend day of travel. Tell where you went and what you saw. Write about unusual things —things that made your trip memorable.

Painters make pictures with paints and brushes. Other artists use crayons, charcoal, and colored pencils to make pictures. Writers make pictures too. They use *words* to make pictures.

Think of your favorite place to be. Make a picture of it with *words*. Tell where it is, how you get there, what it looks like, what sounds you hear, what things you smell, and what you see when you are there. How do you feel when you are there?

I like to be

_____

_____

_____

_____

_____

_____

_____

Sometimes you have so many good writing ideas that you're afraid they'll disappear if you take time to write them in long sentences.

So that you won't forget your great ideas, you can quickly make a list of *words* to save them. Then you can go back and write sentences and paragraphs.

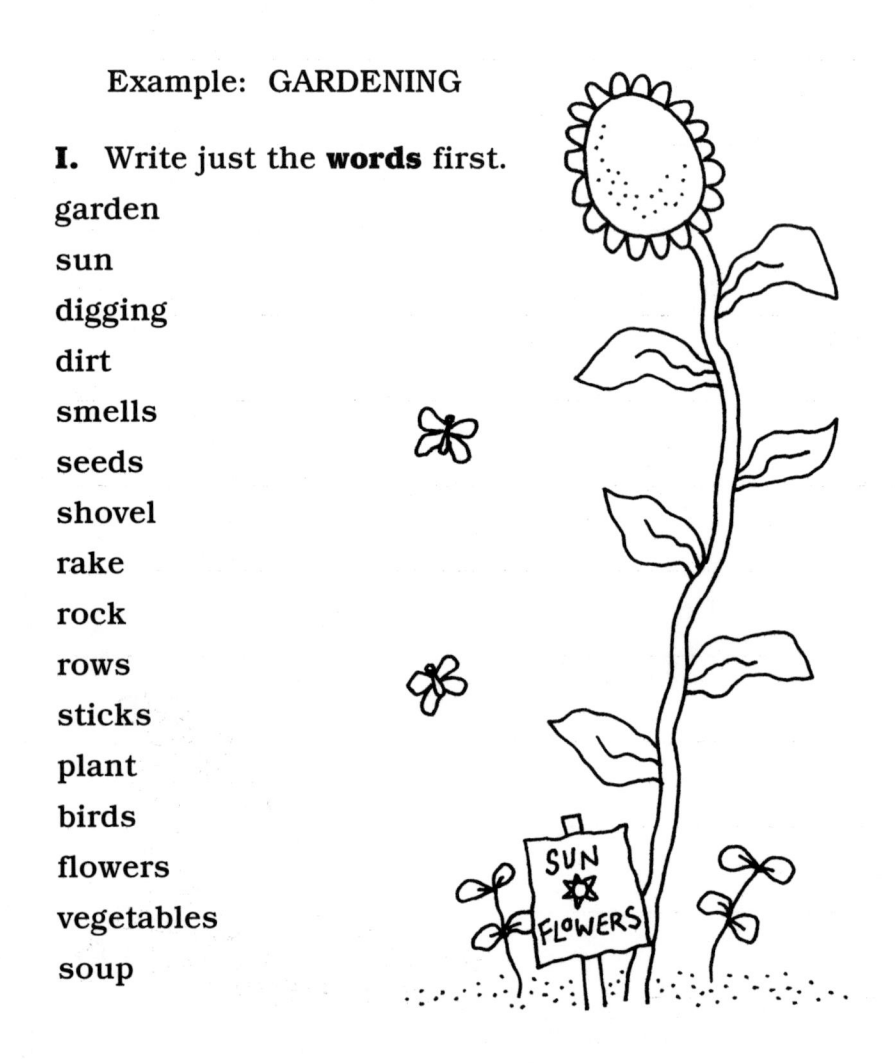

Example: GARDENING

I. Write just the **words** first.
garden
sun
digging
dirt
smells
seeds
shovel
rake
rock
rows
sticks
plant
birds
flowers
vegetables
soup

II. Now go back to the words and write sentences.

Gardening

I love to be out in the **sun**, **digging** in my **garden**. When I dig into the black **dirt**, it **smells** fresh and new.

First I dig with my **shovel**. Next I **rake** it smooth and take out the **rocks**.

Then I **plant** tiny **seeds** that will grow into pretty **flowers** and delicious things to eat.

I plant long, straight **rows** and fasten a string to **sticks** at each end so I can see where I made the rows.

While I am gardening, **birds** watch and sing to me. I think they are happy, too, that soon there will be flowers to see and **vegetables** to eat. Then we will make my favorite vegetable **soup** and I will eat bowls and bowls and bowls of it!

~~garden~~   ~~dirt~~
~~sun~~   ~~smells~~
~~digging~~   ~~seeds~~

* Cross out words in your list as you use them up. Add other ideas as you think of them.

Now **you** choose something! Maybe you will write about walking or roller skating, about playing soccer or making a snowman. Perhaps you want to write about your hobby. Turn the page and start writing. Remember: first make your word list, then write sentences.

Word List

Sentences

Important people often write their *memoirs*. That's a fancy word that means the things they remember.

You are important too! Write your own *memoirs*. Think of the very first thing you can remember. Now write about it.

On the last pages of your book, write whatever you wish.

* Remember, the more you practice writing, the better you'll get at it!